HUMAN BODY BOOK
INTRODUCTION TO THE CIRCULATORY SYSTEM
Children's Anatomy & Physiology Edition

SPEEDY PUBLISHING

Speedy Publishing LLC
40 E. Main St. #1156
Newark, DE 19711
www.speedypublishing.com

Copyright 2015

All Rights reserved. No part of this book may be reproduced or used in any way or form or by any means whether electronic or mechanical, this means that you cannot record or photocopy any material ideas or tips that are provided in this book

The heart is one of the only muscles that works in your body without you having to think about it.

The circulatory system is also called the cardiovascular system or the vascular system.

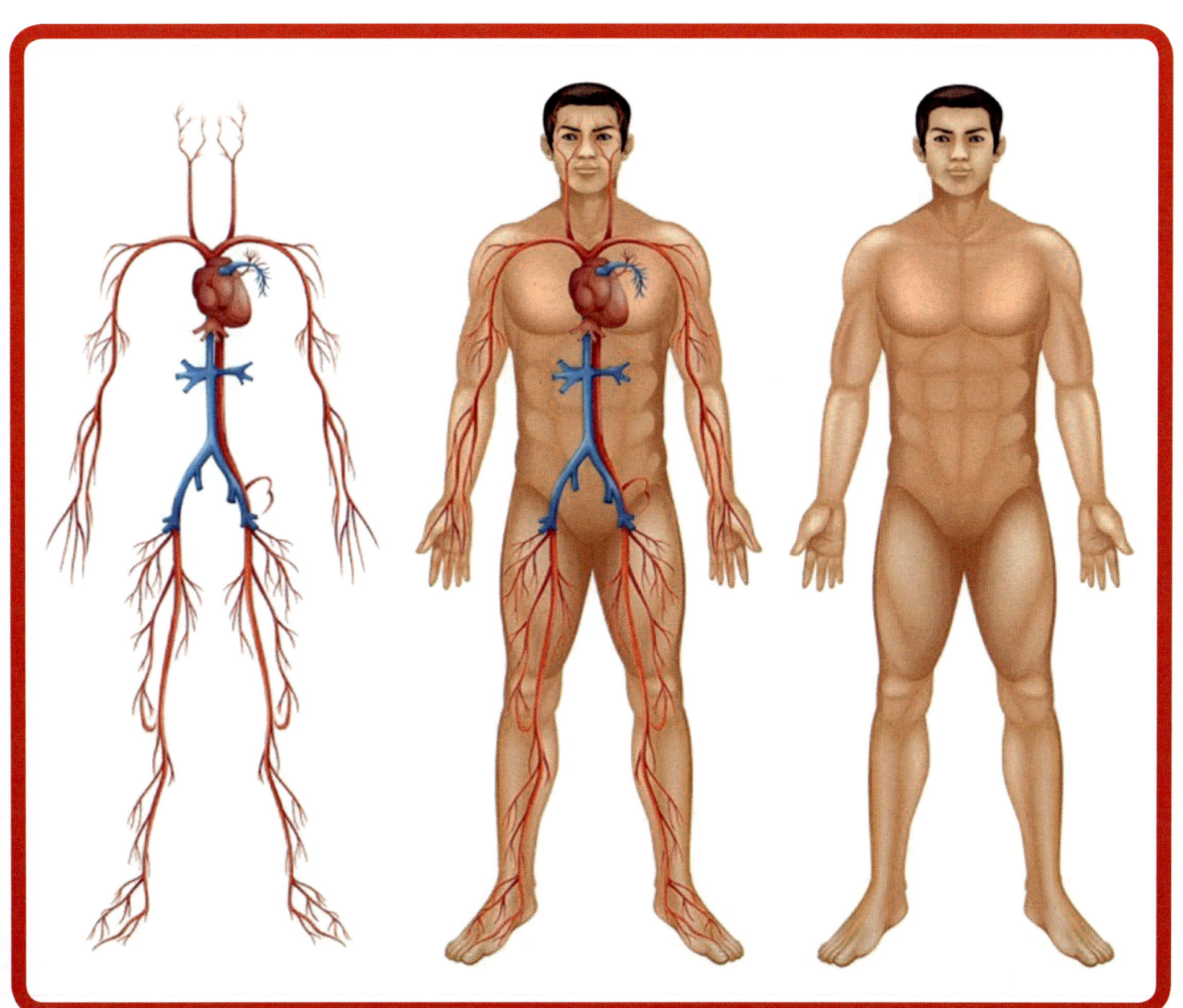

The circulatory system is a vast network of organs and vessels that is responsible for the flow of blood, nutrients, hormones, oxygen and other gases to and from cells.

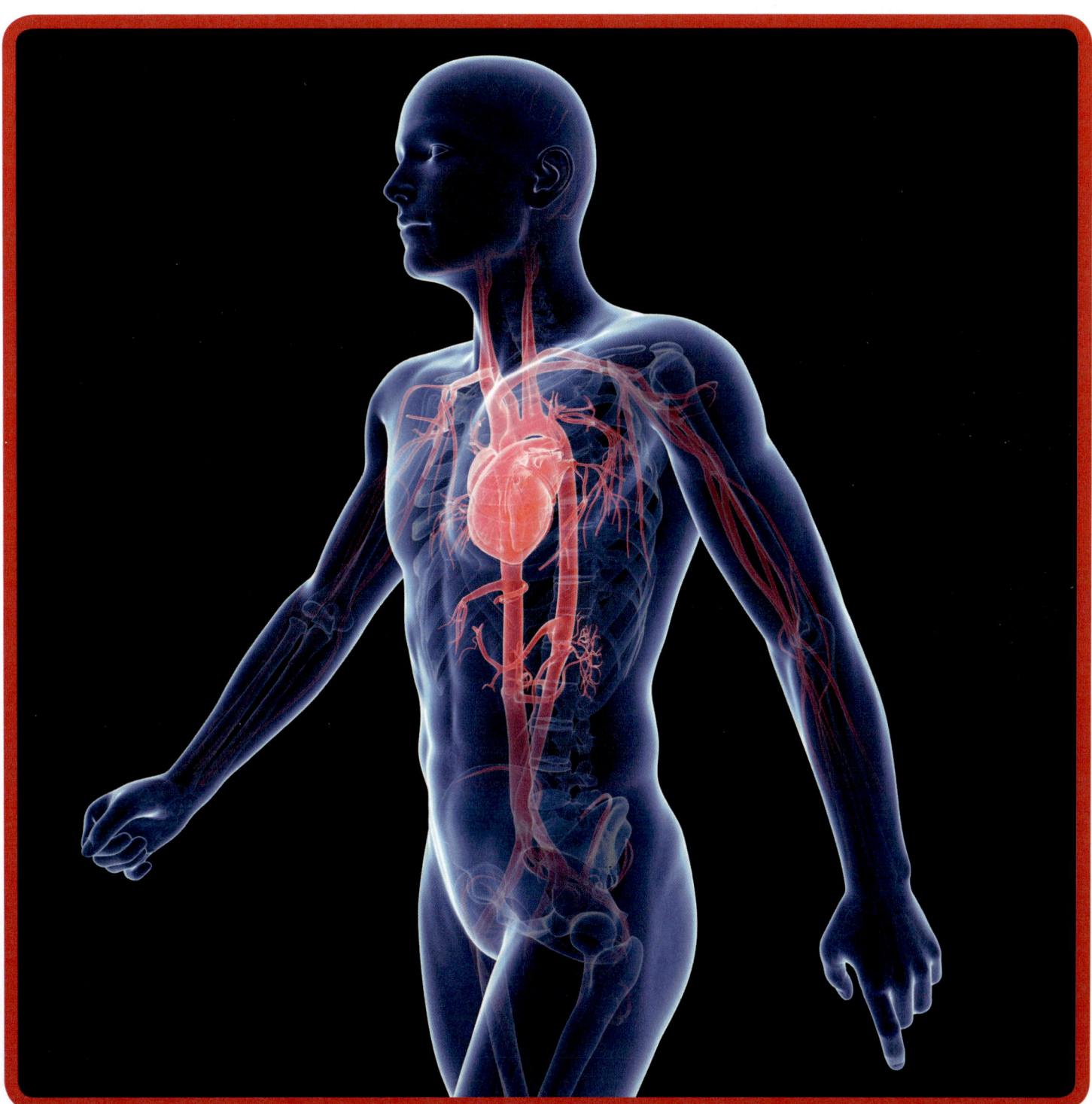

The circulatory system is centred on the heart, a muscular organ that rhythmically pumps blood around a complex network of blood vessels extending to every part of the body.

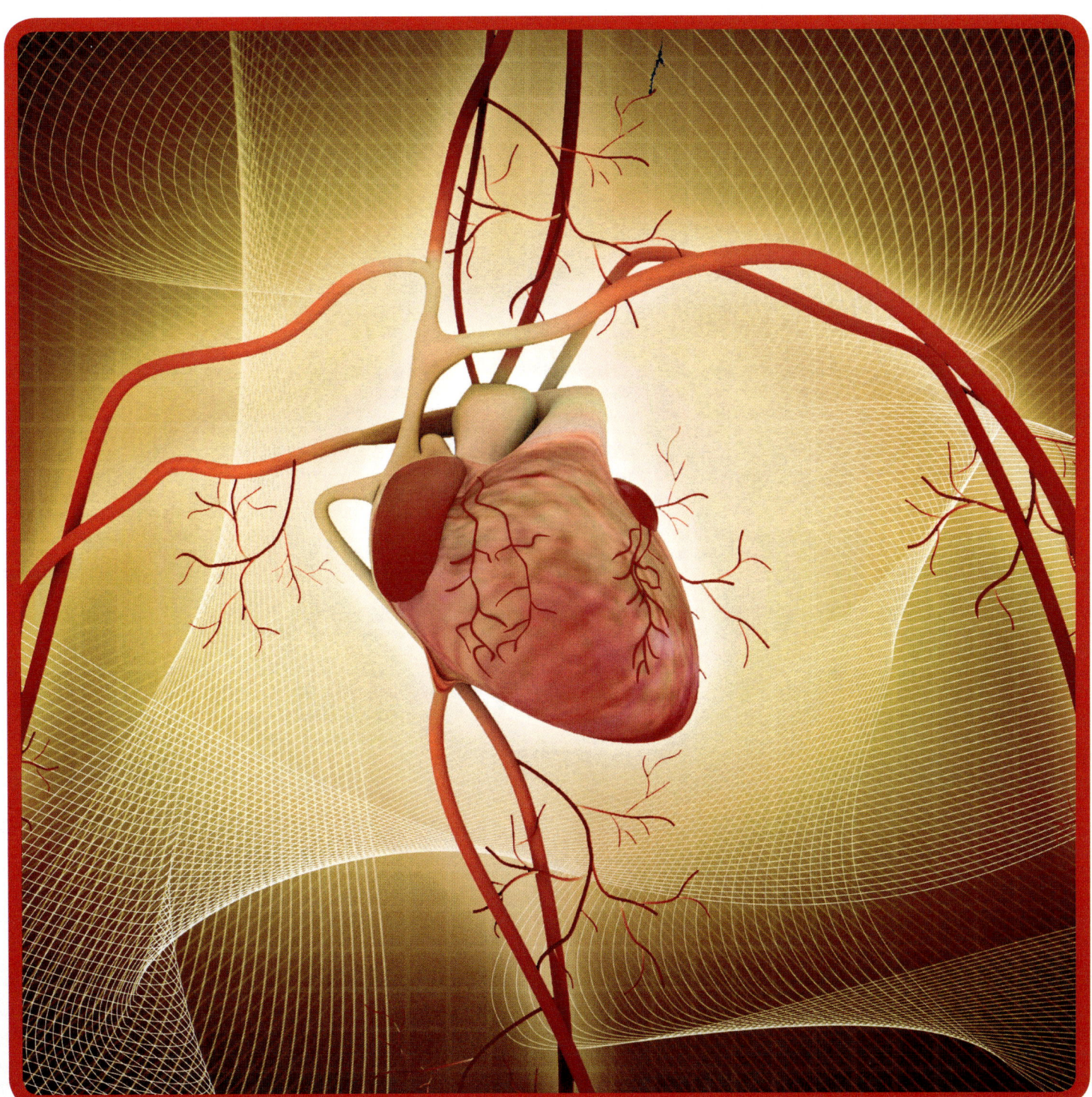

Blood carries the oxygen and nutrients needed to fuel the activities of the body's tissues and organs.

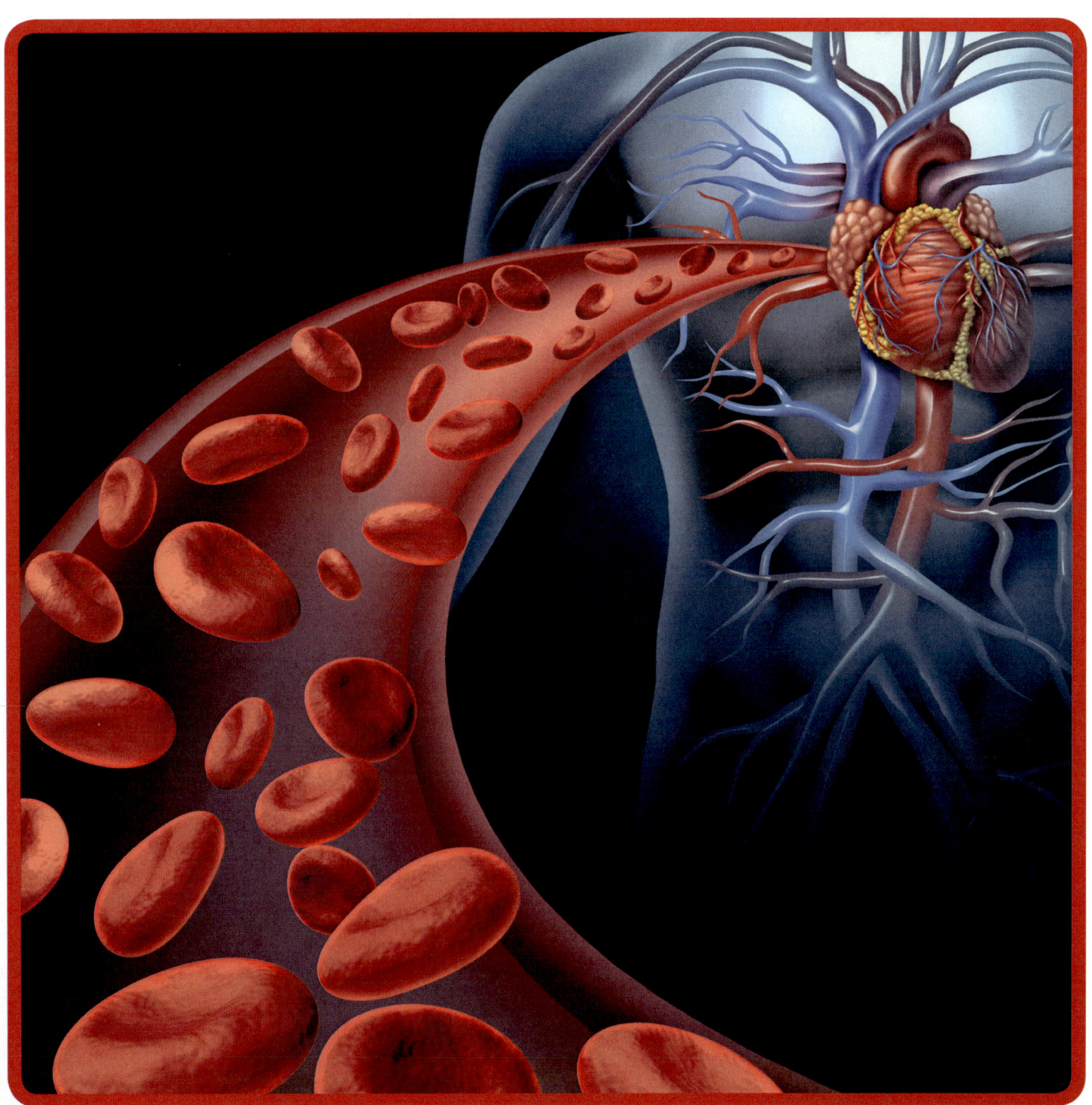

Capillaries are tiny, averaging about 8 microns in diameter, or about a tenth of the diameter of a human hair.

Red blood cells are about the same size as the capillaries through which they travel, so these cells must move in single-file lines.

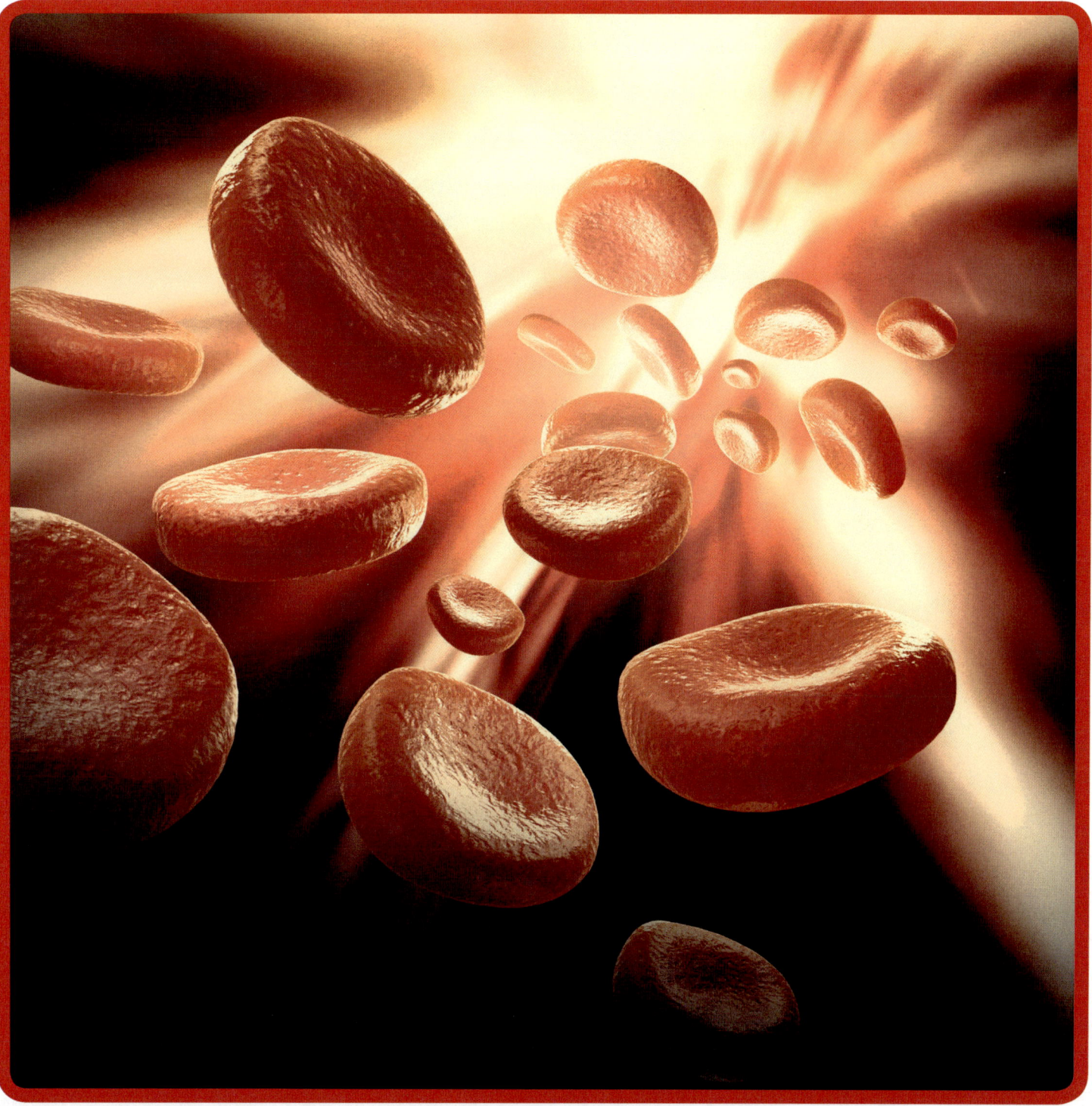

Blood consists of plasma, red blood cells, white blood cells, and platelets.

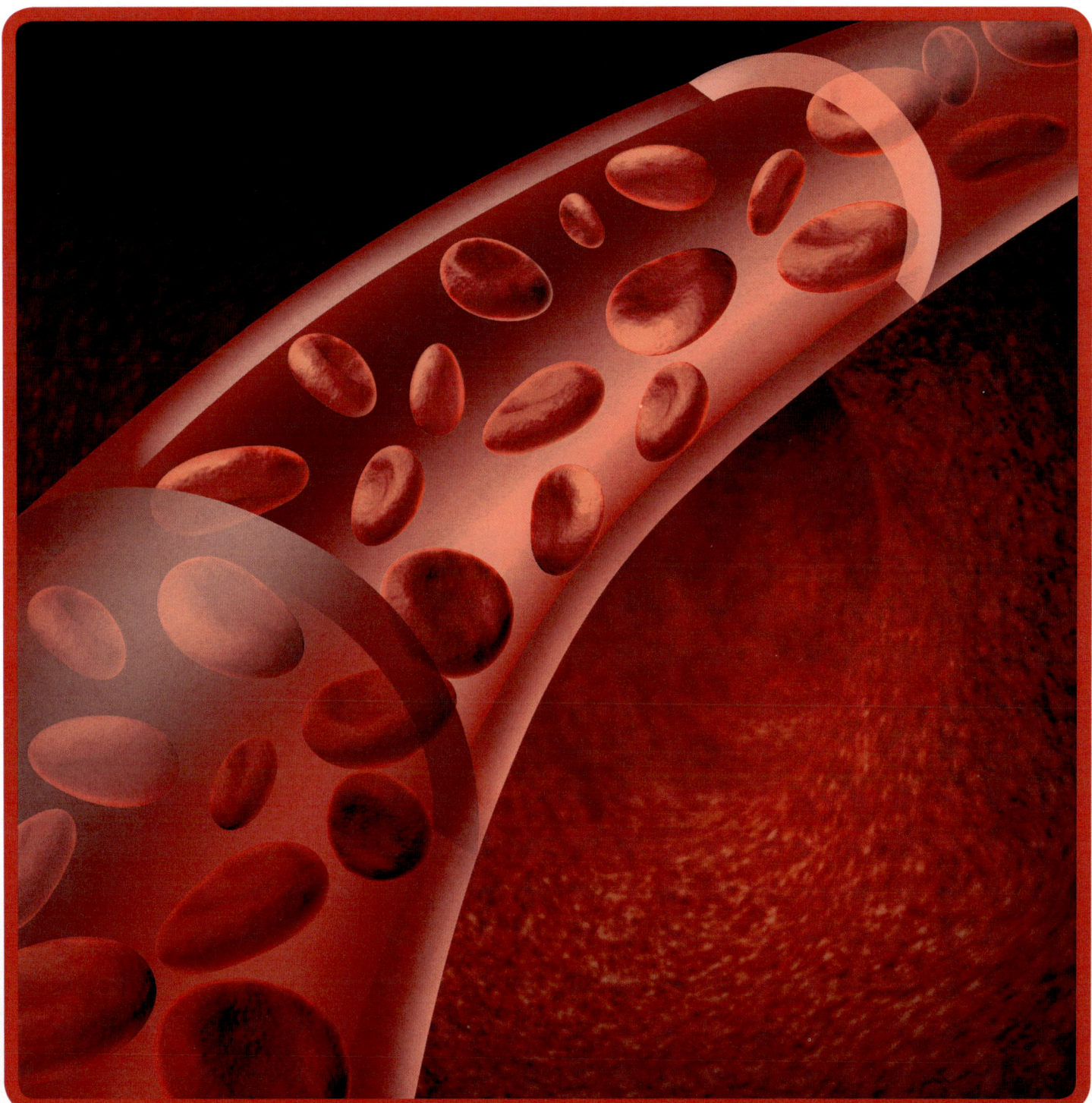

Arteries are blood vessels that carry blood away from the heart.

Arteries have a higher blood pressure than other parts of the circulatory system.

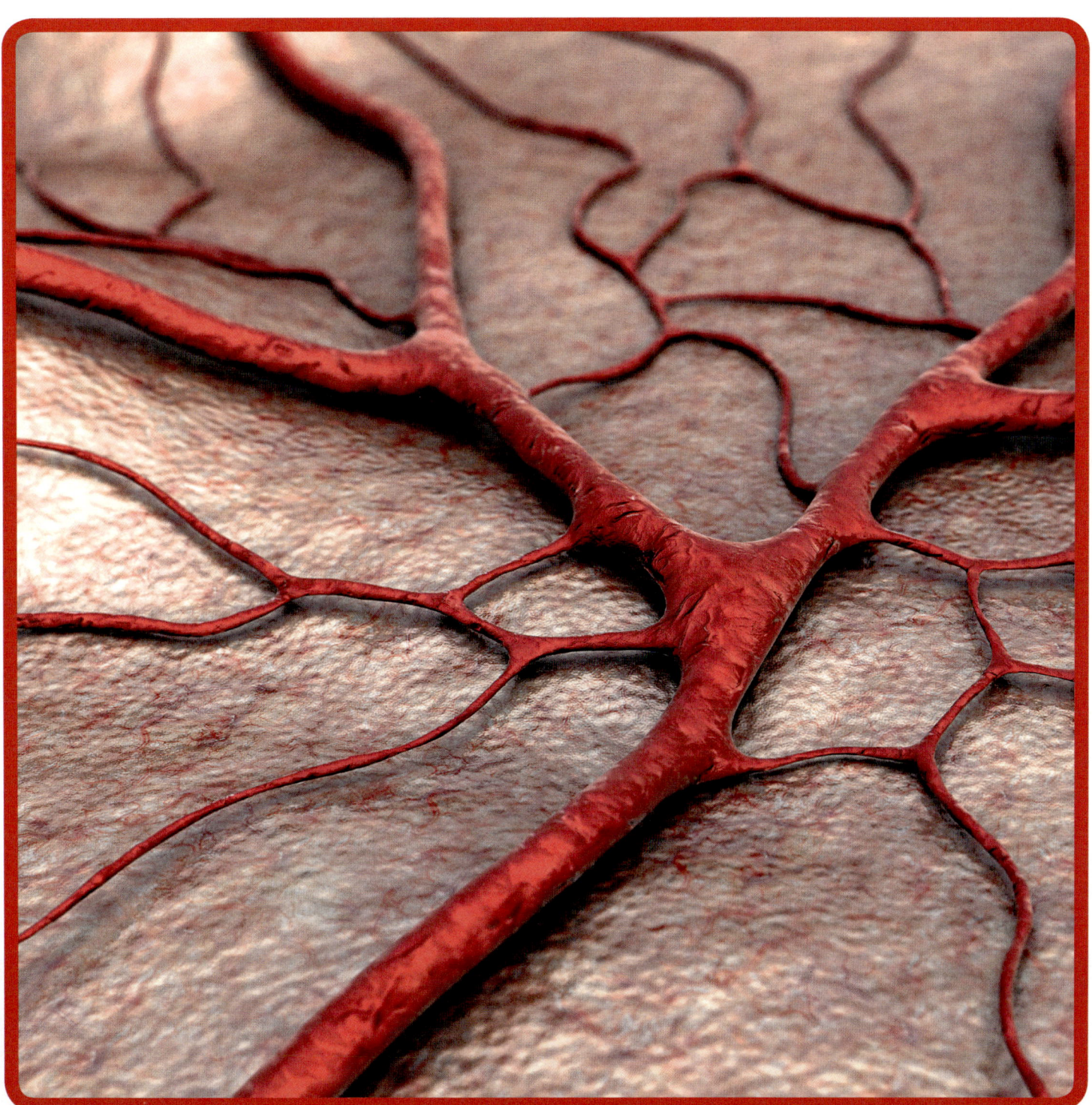

Veins are blood vessels that carry blood toward the heart.

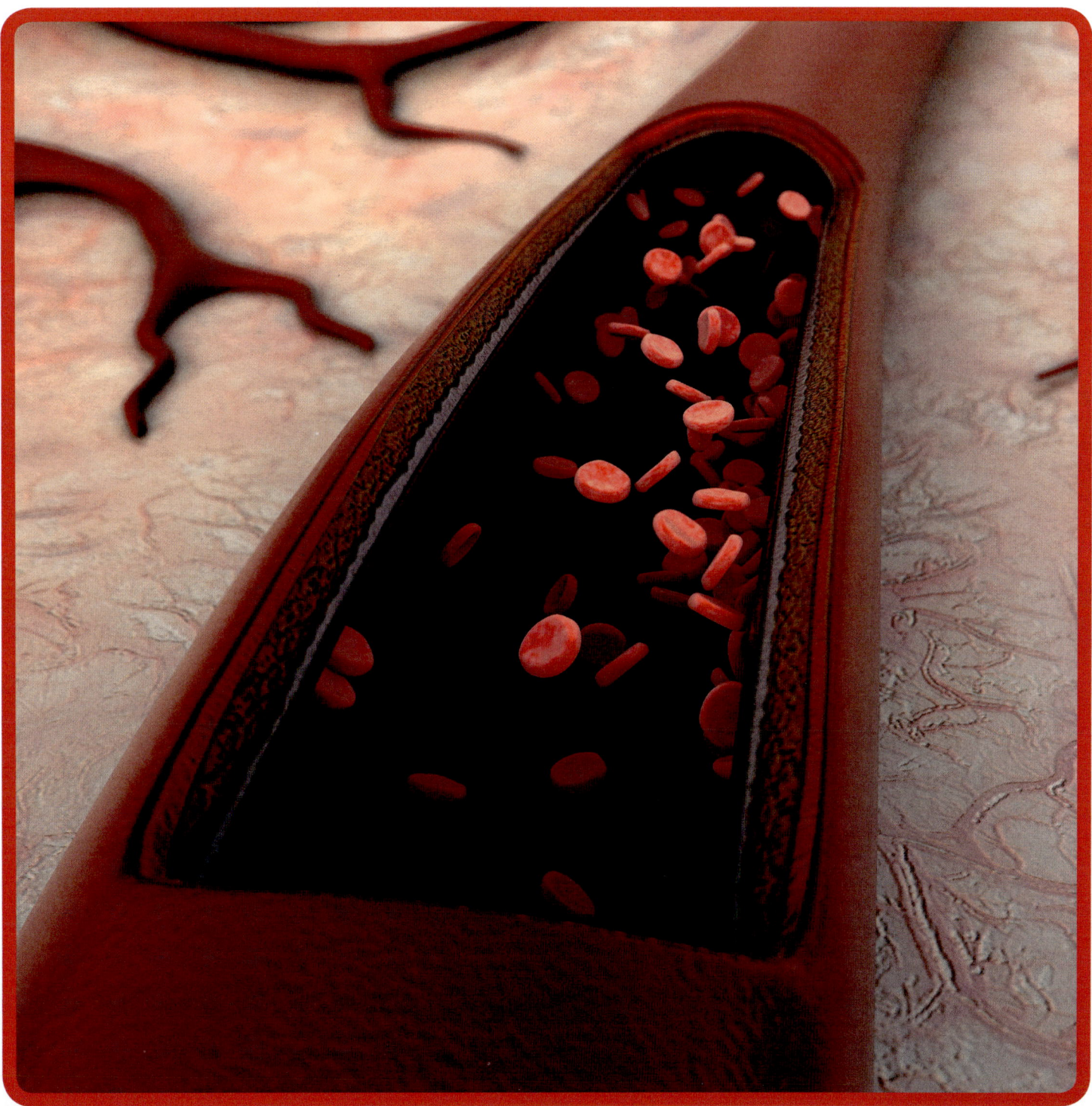

Most veins carry deoxygenated blood from the tissues back to the heart.

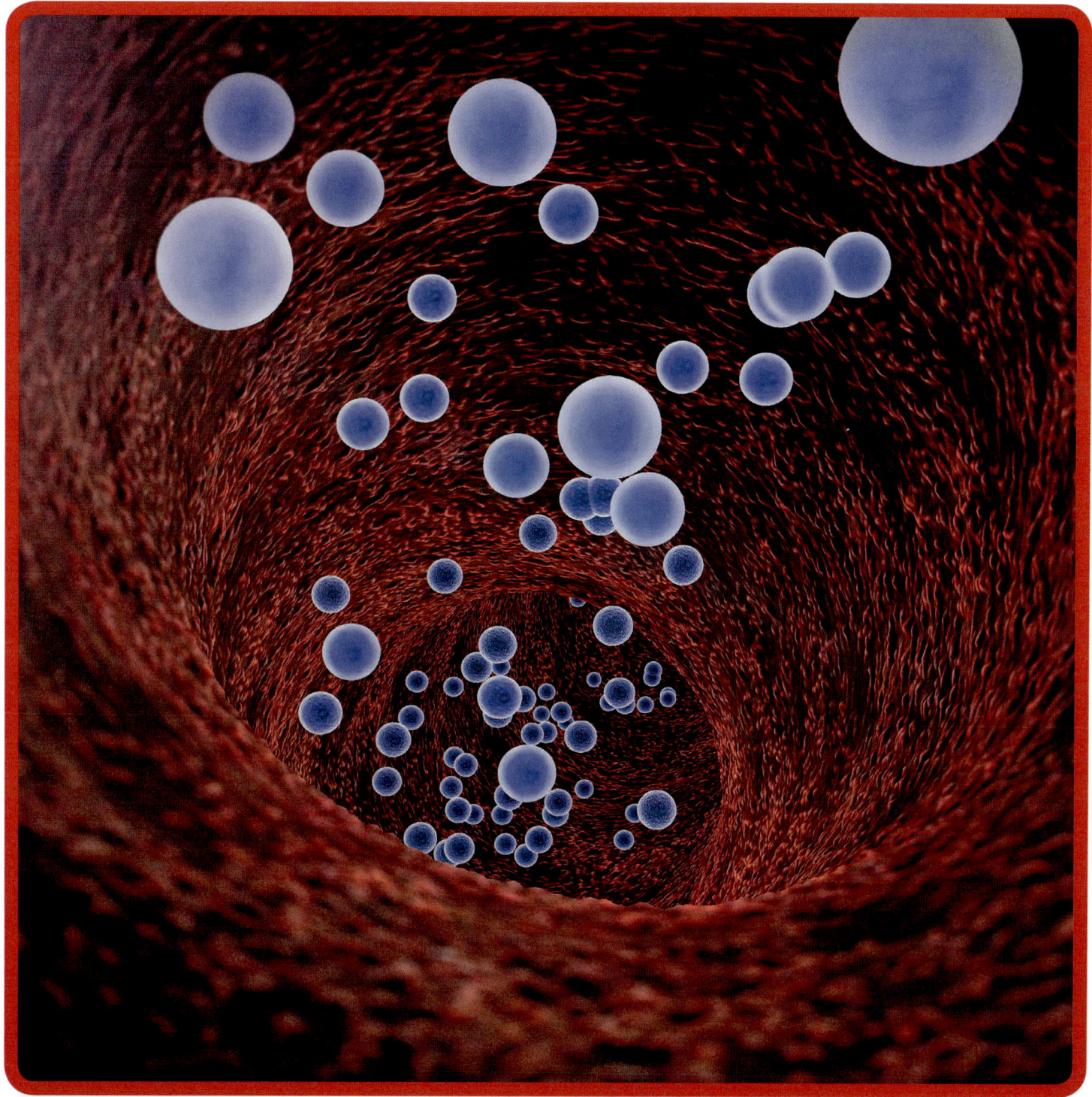

Veins are less muscular than arteries and are often closer to the skin.

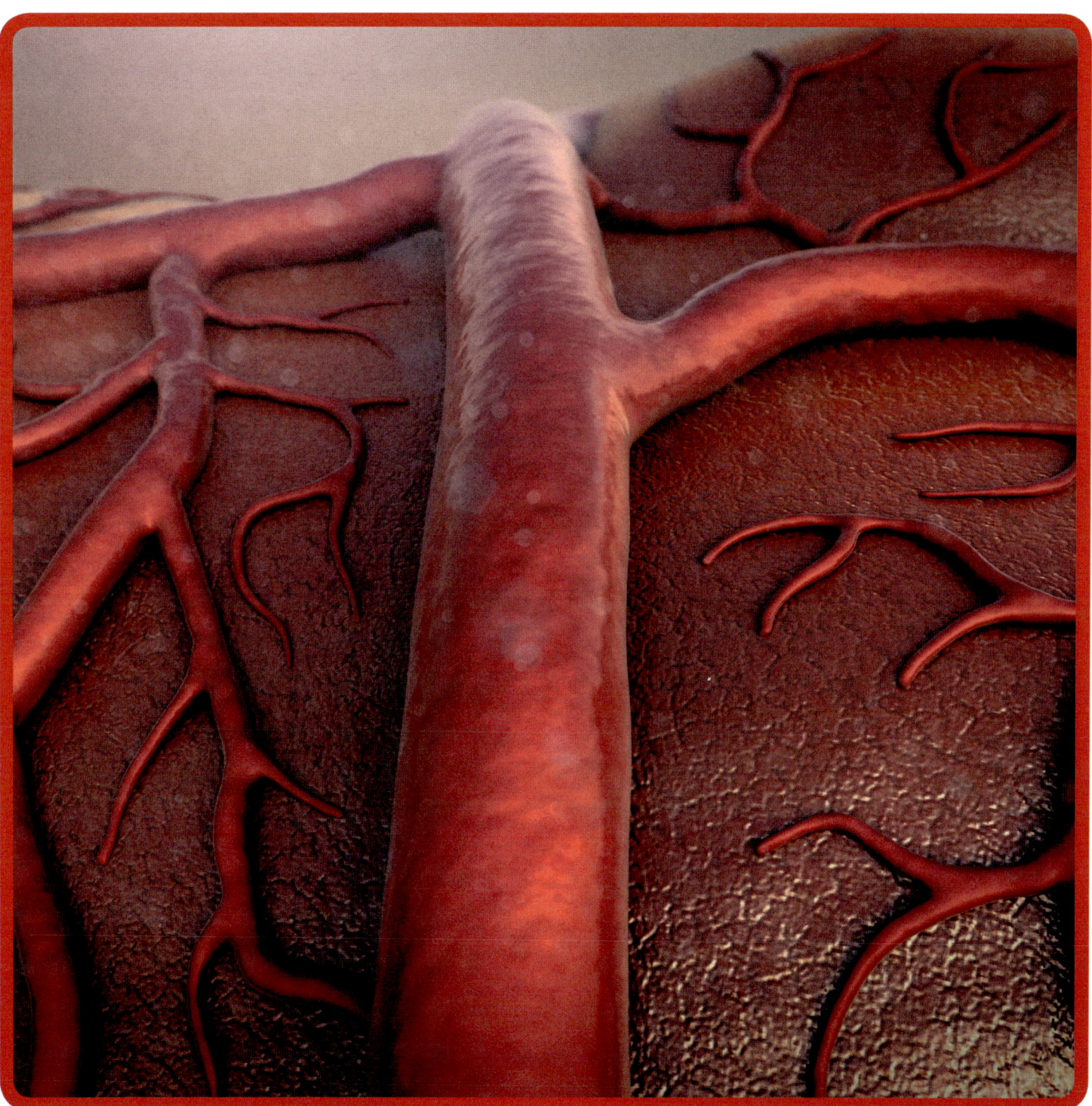

Coronary circulation is the circulation of blood in the blood vessels of the heart muscle.

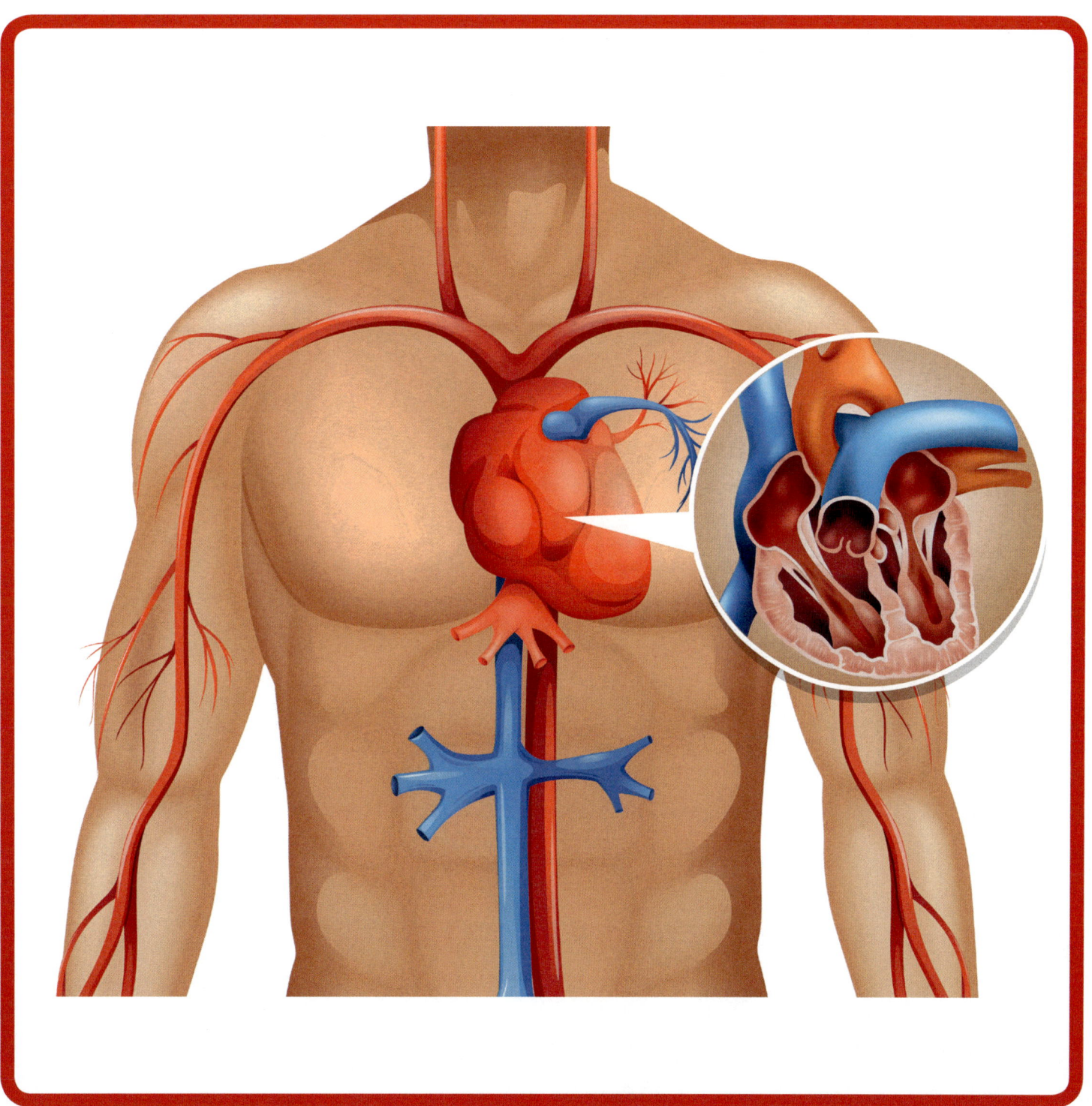

The vessels that deliver oxygen-rich blood to the myocardium are known as coronary arteries.

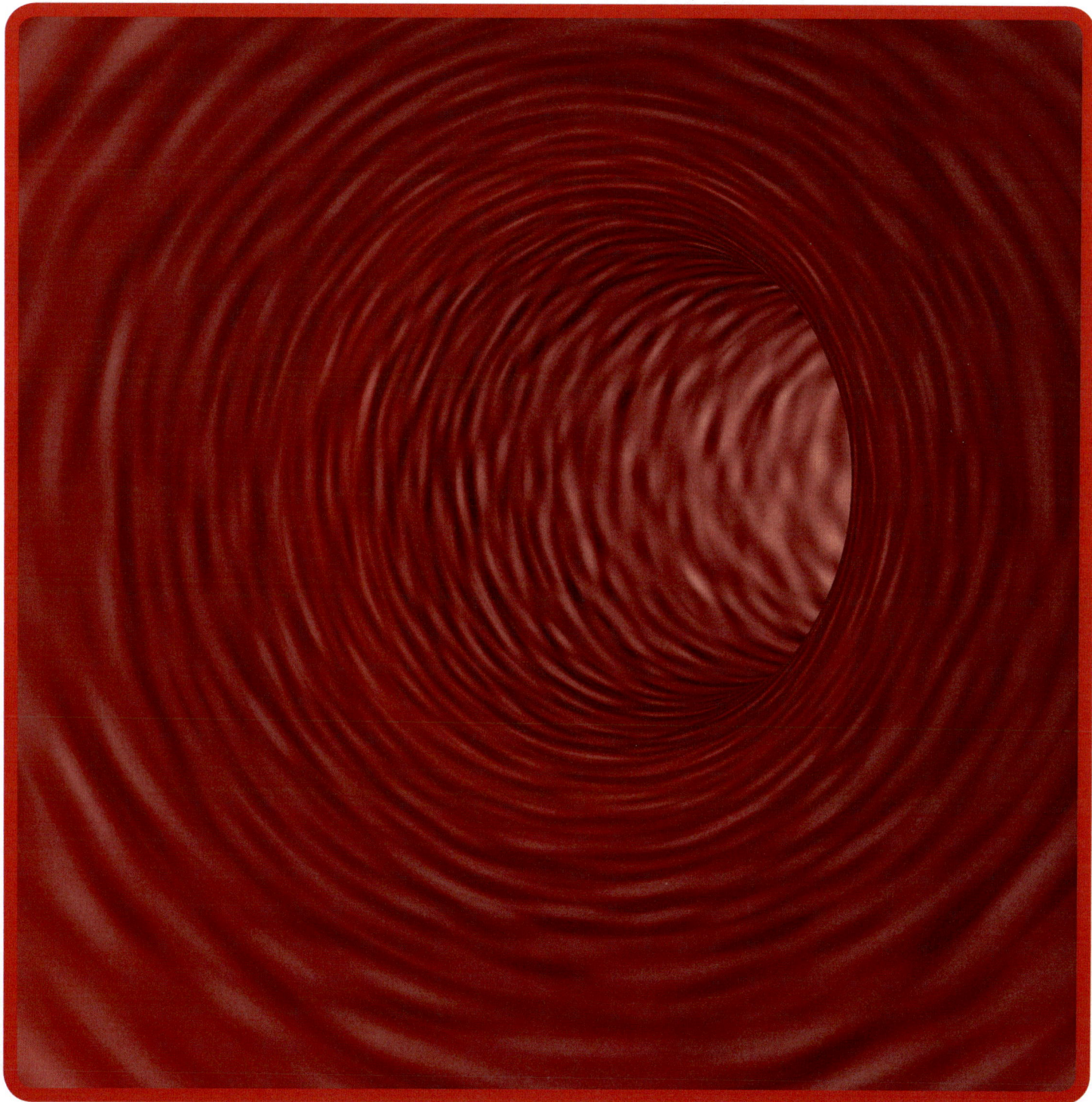

The vessels that remove the deoxygenated blood from the heart muscle are known as cardiac veins.

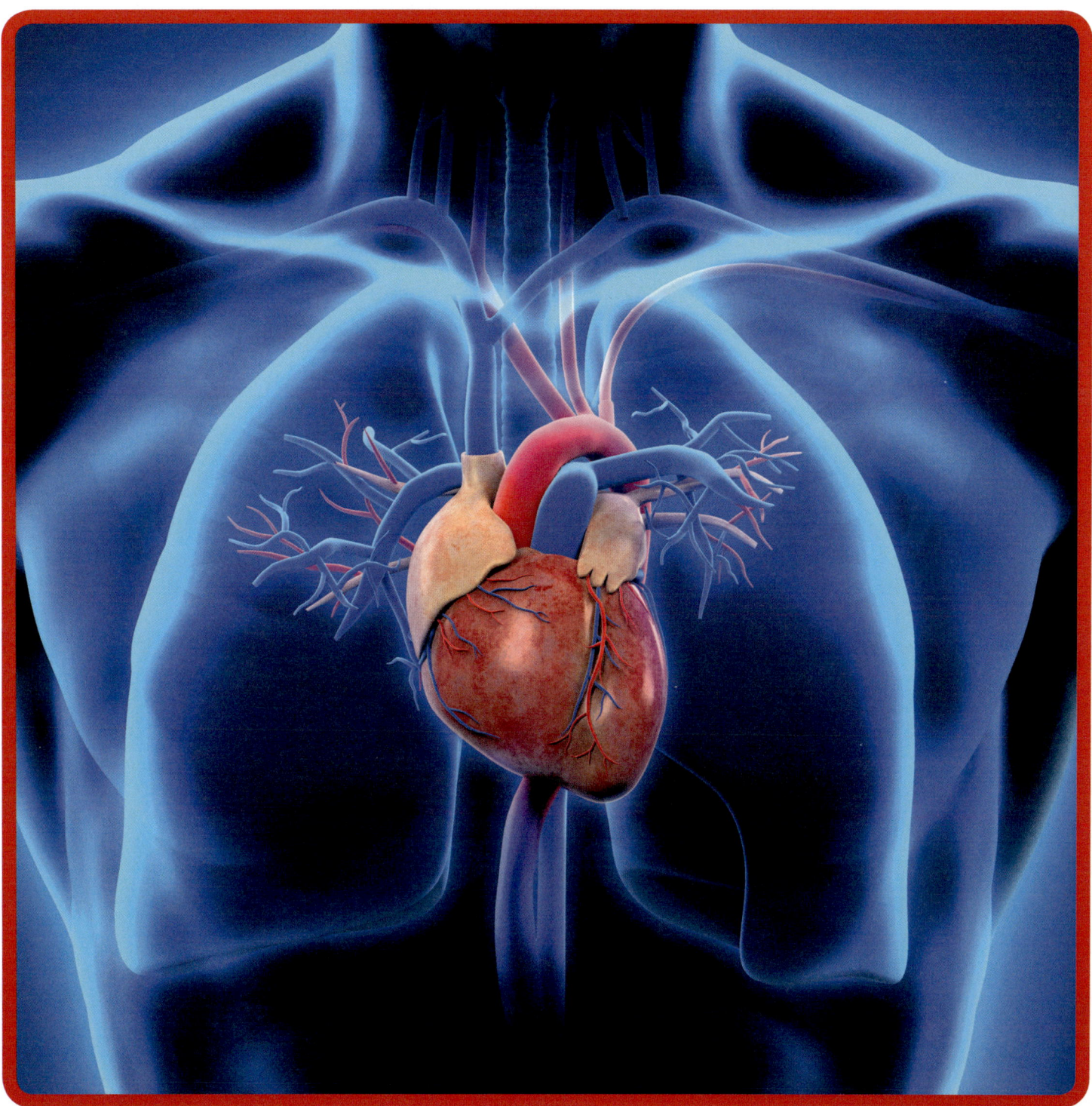

Human blood is colourless, it is the hemoglobin that makes it red.

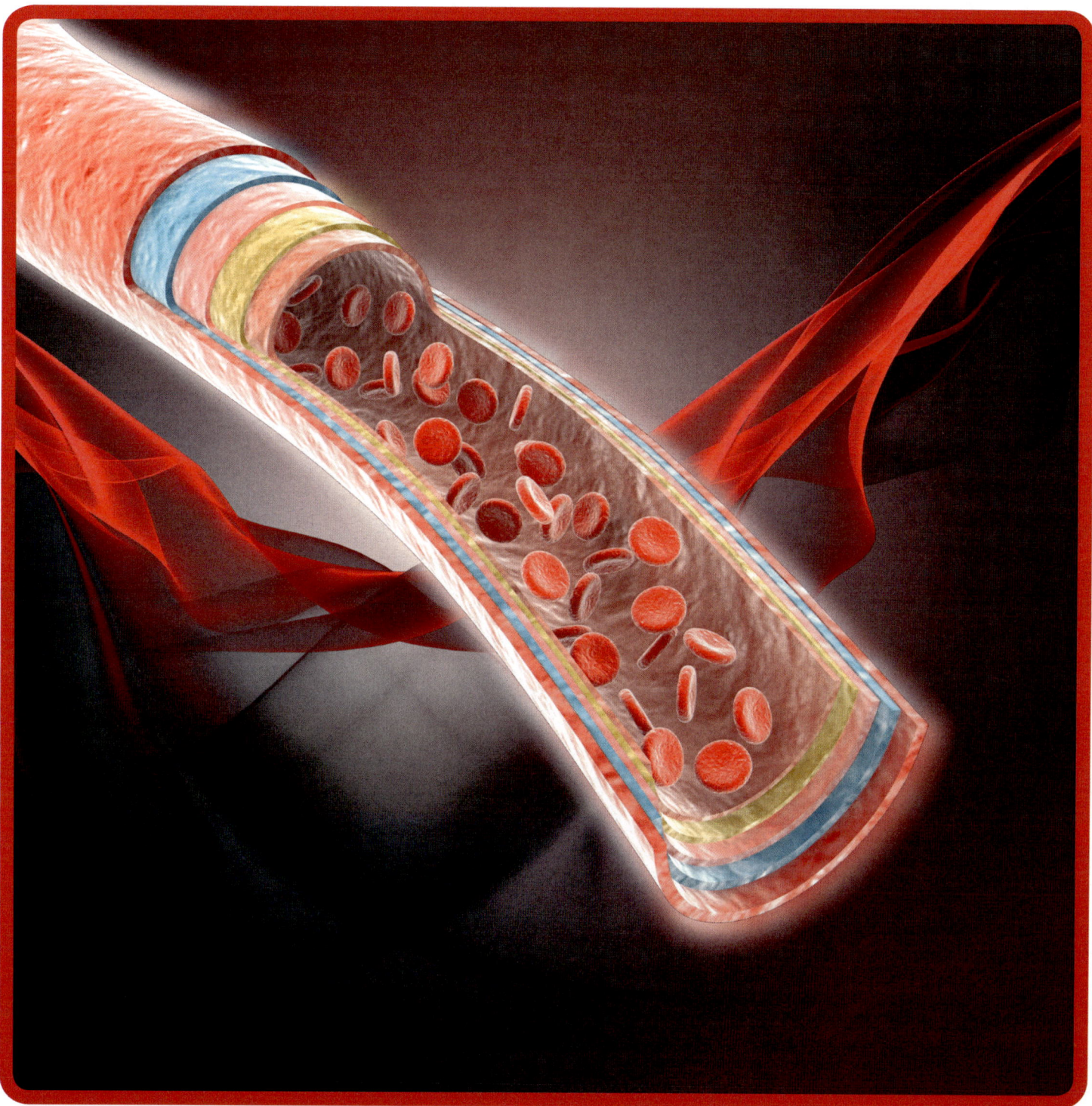

It takes 20 seconds for blood to circulate the entire body. Oxygenated blood leaves the aorta about about 1 mile an hour.

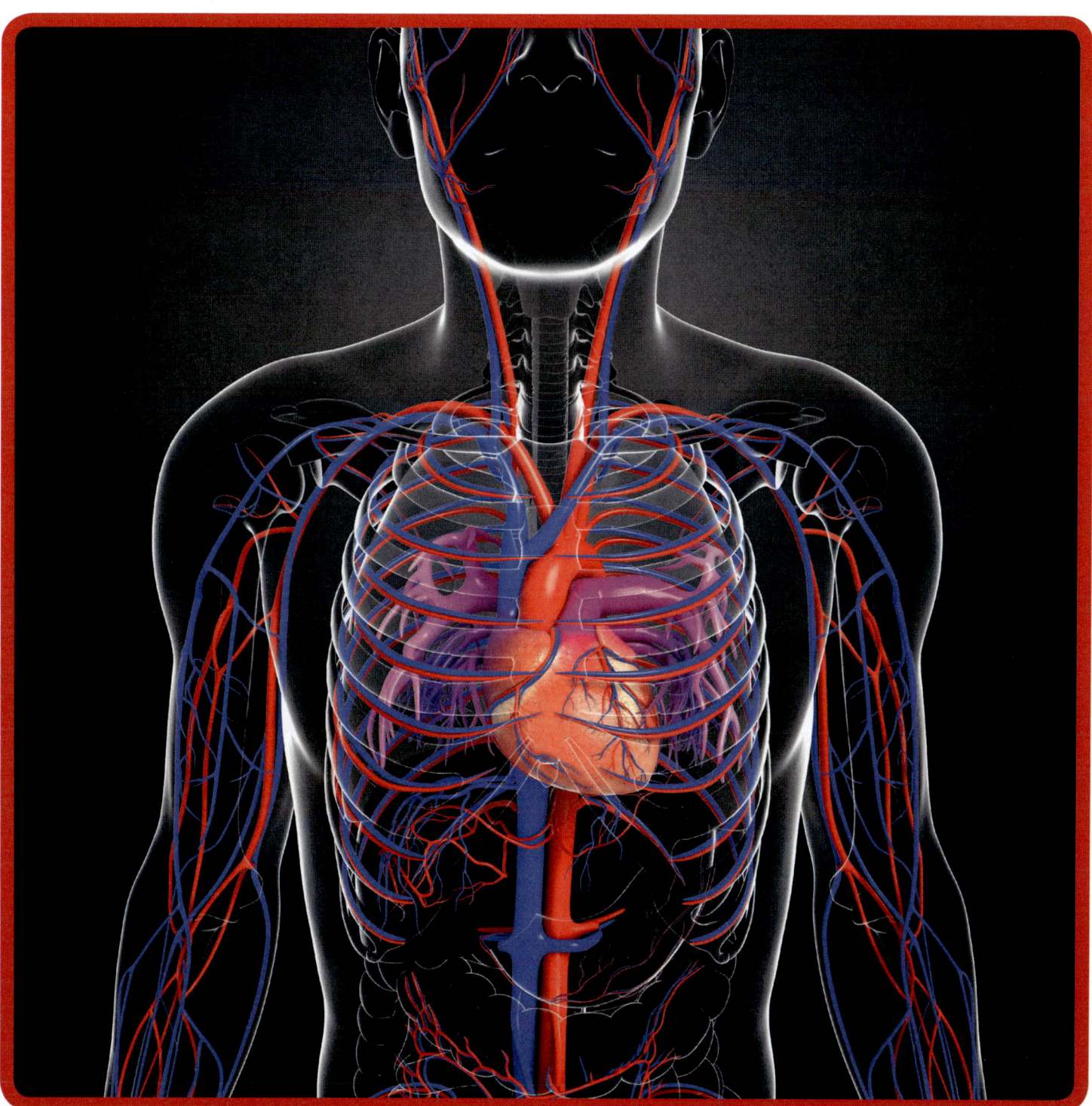

The heart contracts tirelessly – more than 2.5 billion times over an average lifetime – to pump blood around the body.

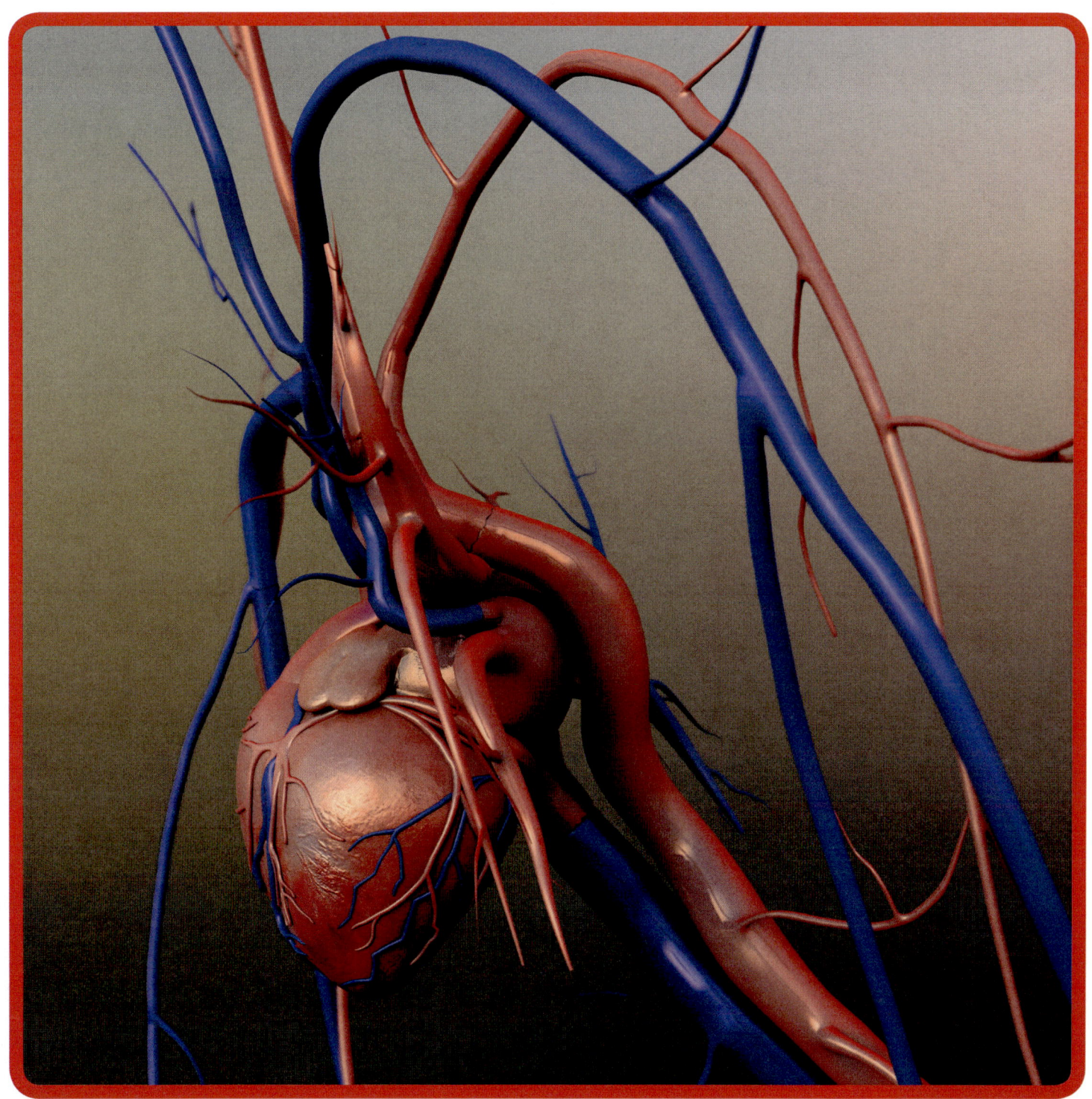

Made in the USA
Coppell, TX
06 October 2023